EVERY THURSDAY
Positive Power XXI Media

A Jerry Royce Production

9PM EST

Made to *Leads*

MILLIONS

PODCAST

COACH KRYSTAL HENRY

NEED MORE EXPOSURE!
Be A Guest On My Program

Contact:

Producer, JerryRoyceLive@gmail.com

Sales Team Guru
#1 SELLING TEAM FOR ENTREPRENEURS

BUILD YOUR 7-FIGURE SALES TEAM *Challenge*

How To Build Your 7-Figure Sales Team Without Spending ONE Dime
To Provide The Revenue To Purchase The Resources Necessary
To Execute The Vision You Have For The People You Were
Called to Serve!

Count Me In: www.BuildYourSalesTeamChallenge.com

DAY 3

HOW TO TRAIN SALES REPS
1:00 - 3:00 PM ET /
10:00 - 12:00 PM PT

DAY 4

SALES AFFILIATE, SALES AMBASSADORS AND DIGITAL SALES SOLUTION TEAM
1:00 - 3:00 PM ET /
10:00 - 12:00 PM PT

STEP 1
UNLOCK THE POWER OF A 7-FIGURE SALES TEAM & SERVE THOSE WHO NEED YOU MOST

STEP 2
SIMPLIFY THE TECHNOLOGY & INCREASE YOUR REVENUE

STEP 3
LAUNCH YOUR KNOWLEDGE, EXPERTISE, PRODUCT OR SERVICE TO THE WORLD AND CREATE A MOVEMENT

I'm Ready: www.BuildYourSalesTeamChallenge.com

WHEN YOU JOIN THE BUILD YOUR 7-FIGURE SALES TEAM CHALLENGE FOR FREE RIGHT NOW YOU'LL GET:

5 days of live trainings starting Day ONE at 1pm EST (same time daily) with Che Brown & surprise guests that will blow your mind!

Access to our private Facebook group exclusively for the Build Your 7-Figure Sales Team challenge. You'll be eligible to win amazing prizes daily inside the group including Close Conference tickets, signed copies of Che's book, Client Winning Sales Funnel Blueprint course and more!

Daily assignments that will have you successfully launching your 7-Figure Sales Team to the world in 5 days or less!

Join Now: www.BuildYourSalesTeamChallenge.com

Table of Contents

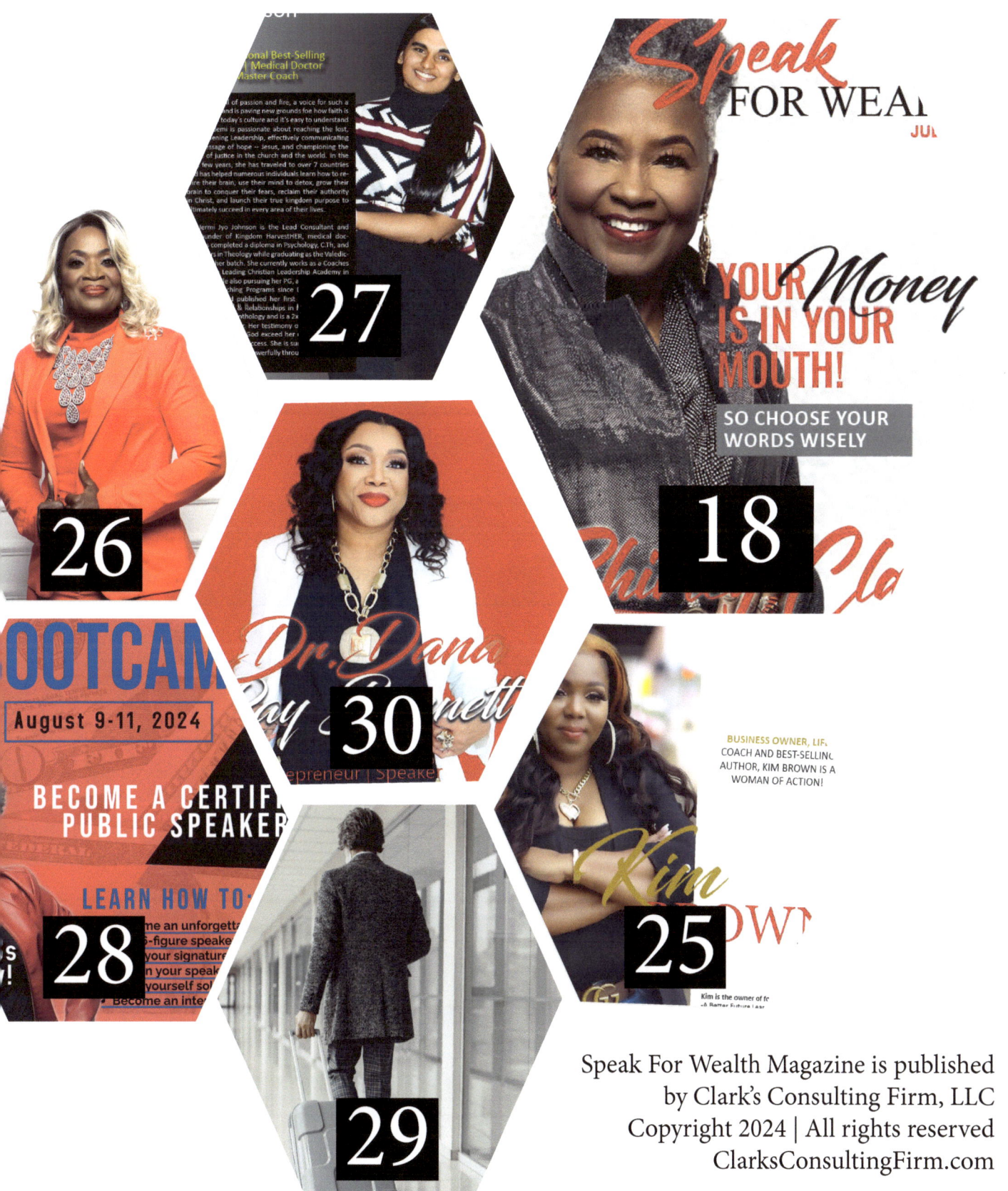

Speak For Wealth Magazine is published
by Clark's Consulting Firm, LLC
Copyright 2024 | All rights reserved
ClarksConsultingFirm.com

Dr. Shirley K. Clark

From the PUBLISHER

Welcome to Speak For Wealth. SFW is a premier magazine dedicated to celebrating the world's most influential and powerful speakers. Our mission is to illuminate the journeys, achievements, and wisdom of extraordinary individuals who inspire and lead through the art of oratory.

Each edition of Speak For Wealth features prominent profiles and exclusive interviews with a diverse array of trailblazers. From renowned celebrities and self-made millionaires to visionary community leaders, global ambassadors, church dignitaries, and marketplace innovators, we spotlight those who have harnessed their voices to effect change and shape the future.

As a high-end publication, Speak For Wealth offers a sophisticated blend of compelling narratives, stunning photography, and insightful commentary. Our readers are invited into the lives and minds of the world's most captivating speakers, while gaining a rare glimpse into their motivations, challenges, and triumphs.

Whether you're seeking inspiration, knowledge, or a deeper understanding of what it takes to stand out on the world stage, Speak For Wealth is your ultimate source. Join us as we celebrate the power of words and the remarkable individuals who wield them with unparalleled grace and impact.

Cindy
HOSKINS

Cindy Hoskins serves her King Jesus in the role of an apostle/prophet with a pioneering and breakthrough anointing to help usher in the King of Glory as He releases the Fire and Glory of His Holy presence. God sends her with a freshly anointed fiery message designed to awaken, purify, and prepare the Bride to rule and reign as priests, kings, and overcomers.

She often travels with the Tabernacle of Fire and Glory -- a visual representation of the types and patterns of heaven that sets the atmosphere for intimate worship and a glorious open heaven. People are ushered into the all-consuming light of His Holy presence and undergo life changing transformation.

Cindy speaks and minisiters at numerous conferences, prayer events, churches, and leaders' meetings, both nationally and internationally. She has authored and released many cutting edge teachings that unveil the pure and true image of Jesus, calling all to return to the LORD! Multitudes are challenged and empowered.

Learn more, please visit:

www.PureImageInternational.org

Highlights From
The Grace, Grit and
Glory Experience

NEW BOOK RELEASE

About the Author

My name is Melissa, and I am a mother of three boys, a step-mother to one, and a loving wife. I have been in the medical field for 14 years and helping others is a passion of mine. I have earned my CHT and CCHT licenses as a Hemodialysis Technician, CNA Phlebotomist and OSHA Safety Officer certifications. Currently, I take care of my mother through hospice, and she is being moved over to home health care. I independently manage a private Home Healthcare agency and I am a property owner! I have developed a love for writing and hope it will be a career in my future. I believe there is no life without God, and no life worth living without love, and no life without trial, so stay humble.

Contact Information:
Melissaangel81@yahoo.com

Available on Amazon

Melissa PADILLA LUJAN

Dr. Bridgette B.
JOHNSON

Best-Selling
AUTHOR

Destiny
STRATEGIST

Keynote
SPEAKER

About Dr. Johnson

Dr. Bridgette B. Johnson is an enthusiasts that enjoys helping people discover their purpose, passion, and gifting in order to pursuit their dreams and destiny in life. For over 30 years, Dr. Johnson has been a catalyst for change regardng life challenges that has a stumbling affect on a person at first until the gems of he storm are discovered. Once the is revealed, it will make th epathway for healing and restoration in the life of rhe individual. Dr.BridgetteJohnson@gmail.com

LYNESA'S personal journey of conquering adversity has ignited a deep passion within her to help others. As a Holistic Health Practitioner, Certified Juice Therapist, and Certified Life & Business Coach, she utilizes her expertise to empower individuals to embrace their authentic selves and transform their mindset and unhealthy practices. Through her transformative nine-week weight loss program, "The BellaBody," which is rooted in biblical principles, Lynesa guides others towards holistic health and personal growth, inspiring them to reach their full potential. Beyond her impressive professional accomplishments, Lynesa cherishes her role as a mother and grandmother, recognizing the profound value of family. Her personal experiences, combined with her wealth of expertise, make her an extraordinary source of inspiration for those seeking success in their own lives. Lynesa Williams is not only an accomplished author and the visionary behind "The BellaBody," but she is also a true beacon of hope and motivation. Her incredible journey stands as a testament to the incredible power of personal growth and the indomitable resilience of the human spirit. With her unwavering determination and unwavering support, Lynesa continues to uplift and inspire others on their path to holistic health, personal growth, and unparalleled success.

The BellaBody
MINDSHIFTING TO A BEAUTIFUL BODY

A 9-WEEK COURSE

The BellaBody is a 9 week Biblically based program transforming the weight-loss industry by transforming individuals from the inside out. See, it's not about the food pers-say, it's not dieting or exercising - what it's really about is the changing of a mindset. See, where your mind goes your LIFE and BODY can't help but to follow.

Most exciting are the results. Most people:
- Loss 15-20 pounds and keep it off
- Doscover their true meaning and purpose and begin turning their dreams into reality and most importantly finally
- Discover that true SELF LOVE looks like personally.

The BellaBody

9 WEEKS TO CREATING A BEAUTIFUL BODY THAT REPRESENTS YOUR MIND BODY & SOUL

LYNESAL.. WILLIAMS
THE BELLABODY CREATOR

Testimonies

Hi Lynesa, this is Paula. I just want to thank you so so much for the BellaBody program. I still read the book and have some of the affirmations in my bathroom mirror...I have come a long way mentally & physically...I just want to say thank you & I love you very much for all you have done for me even those things I did not share in the Bella group Happy Holidays to you & your family. You are such an inspiration to me more than you would ever know.

Paula G., RN

Lynesa has been a very inspirational woman to me. She has shown herself to be one who cares about helping others to achieve their highest potential. She's a go getter and loves to lift others up as they climb the latter of success. If one doesn't make it, it's not because she didn't give of her time and her knowledge to make sure you know what she knows. It's a pleasure to know her and know that her heart and her coaching is one I can count on for advice and guidance.

Rosemary Blevins

People decide to lose weight for a variety of reasons. Certainly for me, health is always the overriding factor. But in May 2015, I decided I truly needed to do something about my weight because my daughter was getting married in July. I contacted Lynesa Williams because I remembered her talking about her own weight loss journey and because I knew she understood the physical AND the spiritual components that needed to be addressed.

Rev. Marilynn S. Robinson

YOUR *Money*

Is In Your Mouth

As a professional speaker, no other statement can be truer than, "Your Money is in Your Mouth."

Number one world-renowned speaker, Les Brown says it this way, "You must connect so you can collect."

Professional speakers are storytellers in the marketplace. How well you connect with your audience when you speak will affect your bottom line.

Storytelling is an art and you must master this art to move your audience to want more.

What does more look like?
- More money in your bank account
- More products sold
- More speaking engagements

- More coaching clients
- More brand exposure

You cannot afford as a professional speaker to not hone your speaking skills.

Invest in yourself!

Throughout my speaking career, I have invested numerous hours in trainings, watching videos, listening to CDs and reading books to enhance and hone my speaking skills. And many of these trainings were paid opportunities.

In Myron Golden's book, Trashman to Cashman, there is a saying I live by. In fact, it is my mantra in life -- "Rich people educate themselves; poor people entertain themselves."

You must be a lifelong learner to acquire wealth from your speaking career. I tell my coaching and business clients all the time, remember, "You cannot outearned me until you outlearned me."

When you learn new information, your value goes up in the marketplace. So, since I am believing for major opportunities to open for me, and I desire to travel (first class and on private jets), I either need more relationship currency in my life that can assist with opening these opportunities or I need more money or additional skillsets to make it happen. You have to prepare for greatness!

Inside of everyone are seeds of greatness, and it is what we do with these seeds that

determines our outcome. In life, there will be ebbs and flows, ups and downs, but never let transitions take you out of the game. In fact, you should see these transitions as transformational opportunities.

When you invest in yourself and upgrade your skillsets, you are signaling to the universe that you are ready for more. Everyone has a capacity for increase. It is called growing; it is called stretchmarks. Always be in a place where you are constantly elevating your brain cells with information. Every day I learn something new. Be intentional about your money increase.

As I close, here is a critical point you must understand: Volume does not equal value! There is a saying, "Talking loud saying nothing." Don't be this type of speaker. Educate yourself; hone your speaking skills. **Remember, you are paid for your knowledge, experience, and skillsets.**

About Dr. Shirley K. Clark

In both corporate and governmental spheres, the question echoing in boardrooms is, "Where did Dr. Shirley Clark come from?" Emerging from humble beginnings, Dr. Clark has been elevated by divine guidance to become one of the foremost transformative thought leaders of the 21st century. Her extensive leadership experience includes serving on numerous advisory and non-profit boards and being selected in 2023 to spearhead a Presidential Campaign for the United States of America. Dr. Clark has charted a path that has left global leaders from Africa, London, Trinidad, Holland, Kuwait, Canada, and beyond in awe of her exceptional leadership acumen.

Her impressive resume as a graduate of Les Brown's Speaker's Training Program and a SCORE Workshop Presenter extends to speaking at corporate and community events, inspiring the masses, and coaching and training over 30,000 entrepreneurs, speakers, and leaders. Also, as the former Senior Vice-President of a Millionaire Maker Club, Dr. Clark has been instrumental in the creation of over 10 millionaires. She is an International Keynote Speaker, TV/Podcast Host, Certified Master Life & Executive Business Coach, Millionaire Brand Strategist, Celebrity Spiritual Advisor, Chief Soaking Officer (CSO), City Mobilizer, Humanitarian, Philanthropist, Small Business Development Consultant, and an Award-Winning 12x #1 Amazon International Best-Selling Author.

Dr. Clark's influence has also earned her features on over 400 media outlets and the distinguished honor of receiving two Presidential Lifetime Achievement Awards from President Barack Obama and President Joe Biden.

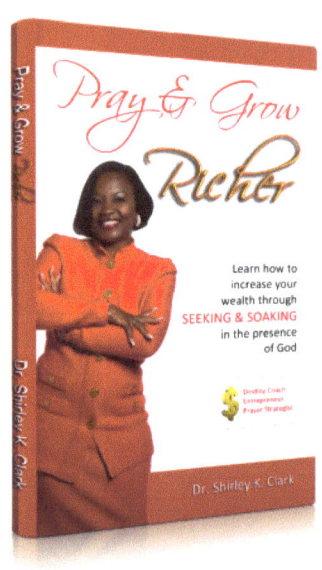

Dr. Clark's full book collection is available on:
www.DrShirleyClark.org

Dr. Clark's Photo Gallery

Rich Mind Rich Life
NEW BOOK RELEASE

Book Description

Preorder your copy today!

AVAILABLE ON
amazon

In "Rich Mind Rich Life," journey with me from the depths of poverty and overwhelming debt to the heights of financial freedom and success. This book is a testament to the power of education, divine intelligence, and relentless self-improvement. Guided by the mantra, "Rich people educate themselves, poor people entertain themselves," I immersed myself in the presence of God and absorbed every book, video, and recording I could find. This path led me to a profound transformation and financial abundance.

As my own finances improved, I felt a calling to help others achieve the same. I created the Pray & Grow Richer 90-Day Mastermind Wealth Program, a powerful coaching strategic training and plan that has been instrumental in creating 11 millionaires. In "Rich Mind Rich Life," you'll meet some of these inspiring individuals and learn how they transformed their lives by changing their mindset.

This book is more than just a memoir; it's a guide to help you shift your perspective, eliminate debt, and achieve financial freedom. Whether you're struggling with debt or looking to elevate your wealth, "Rich Mind Rich Life" offers the insights and tools you need to create a prosperous future.

Are you ready to transform your mind and your life? Dive into "Rich Mind Rich Life" and start your journey to financial freedom today.

To learn more about Dr. Clark, please visit: DrShirleyClark.org

GLOBAL BOOK TOUR

July 2024

Coming to a City Near Your!

10: Virtual Book Launch | Dr. Shirley Live | Pray & Grow Richer Broadcast | Plano, TX

11: Clubhouse Book Discussion | Dallas, TX

12-13: Booksigning | Jungle Birthday Bash | Memphis, TN

16-18: Clubhouse Book Discussion | Dallas, TX

18: Made To Lead Millions Podcast | Carrollton, TX

19: Now Faith Television Show | Los Angeles, CA

20: Jabez Books Zoom Launch | Dallas, TX

21: Clubhouse Book Discussion | Carrollton, TX

23-26: Rich Mind Rich Life Amazon Book Club Rally | Plano, TX

28: Book Signing Reception | St. Louis, MS

Learn more: DrShirleyClark.org

BUSINESS OWNER, LIFE COACH AND BEST-SELLING AUTHOR, KIM BROWN IS A WOMAN OF ACTION!

Kim BROWN

Kim is the owner of four businesses:
-A Better Future Learning Center for 10 years
-Healing Hands Home Healthcare Service
-Divine Purpose Adult Daycare
-Fabulous Fashion Boutique

LEARN MORE:
www.KimBrownEnterprise.com

Dr. Ivy Anderson
Ed.D., D. Min

Dr. Ivy Anderson is a daughter of God, Licensed and Ordained Minister, Prayer Pastor and Co-ordinator for the National Day of Prayer. She is a 4x Amazon Best Selling Author, television producer and host, Licensed Financial Professional, Educational Consultant, Certified Life Coach, Lifewave Leader and Nurse Educator. To fulfill her mandate in life, Dr. Ivy has successfully completed seven earned degrees: Bachelors in Social Work, Nursing and Biblical Studies, Masters in Counseling and Nursing, and Doctorates in Higher Education Administration and Ministry.

Dr. Jemi
Jyo Johnson

International Best-Selling Author| Medical Doctor Master Coach

Dr. Jemi is full of passion and fire, a voice for such a time as this and is paving new grounds foe how faith is engaged in today's culture and it's easy to understand why. Dr. Jemi is passionate about reaching the lost, strengthening Leadership, effectively communicating the message of hope -- Jesus, and championing the cause of justice in the church and the world. In the past few years, she has traveled to over 7 countries and has helped numerous individuals learn how to re-wire their brain, use their mind to detox, grow their brain to conquer their fears, reclaim their authority in Christ, and launch their true kingdom purpose to ultimately succeed in every area of their lives.

Dr. Jermi Jyo Johnson is the Lead Consultant and Co-Founder of Kingdom HarvestHER, medical doctor, has completed a diploma in Psychology, C.Th, and Bachelors in Theology while graduating as the Valedictorian of her batch. She currently works as a Coaches Coach at a Leading Christian Leadership Academy in the U.S. while also pursuing her PG, and has launched multiple Coaching Programs since December 2021. She wrote and published her first book on, "Kingdom Singleness & Relationships in March 2023, has co-authored an anthology and is a 2x #1 International Best Selling author. Her testimony of taking leaps of faith and watching God exceed her expectations has brought her much success. She is such a joy to speak to and God uses her powerfully through her prophetic gift.

SPEAK FOR WEALTH
BOOTCAMP

September 19-21, 2024

BECOME A CERTIFIED PUBLIC SPEAKER

LEARN HOW TO:

- Become an unforgettable speaker
- Be a 6-figure speaker
- Craft your signature message
- Design your speaker's sales packages
- Book yourself solid
- Become an international speaker

VIRTUAL TRAINING
ATTEND FROM THE COMFORT OF YOUR HOME!

LEARN MORE:
WWW.DRSHIRLEYCLARK.ORG

Travel Tips For Speakers

As a professional speaker, here are some great tips to make your travel and speaking experience stress-free as possible

PACK LIGHT: When packing for a trip, start with your essentials for your travel and presentation. Then everything else you pack should be garments that can be rolled up. Usually, a sm/med suitcase and a computer bag or backpack are enough for a 3 to 5-day trip. If you need more space, wear a jacket or garments with pockets that you can substitute for a carry-on. The goal is to take only carry-on bags to avoid waiting at baggage claim. Also, only takes bags with wheels on them.

CHECK THE WEATHER: Please check the weather before dashing off to a speaking engagement in another city, state, or country. You might need a jacket or worst-case scenario, you need to stay home. You don't want to be stuck in an airport or airplane.

ARRIVAL TIME: It is best to arrive a day early to avoid plane delays, cancellations, disruptions, and, possibly, missing your speaking engagements. Also, this will give you time to relax your body and mind as well as prepare for your presentation just in case you forgot to pack something. Don't forget to stay hydrated and eat healthy!

FLIGHT SELECTION: Fly direct flights to reduce the risk of missed connections, delays, and damage luggage. Also, avoid booking flights that are late or the last one. More than likely, there will be delays and your flight will be cancelled.

CONNECTIONS/TRANSFERS: When waiting for connections or transfers in an airport, please constantly check monitors for gate, terminal, and time of flight to avoid being stranded at an airport. These things can change frequently. To help stay up to date, download the airline app onto your phone to receive updates, weather alerts, rebooking info, etc asap.

BACKUP PRESENTATION: Your presentation should be everywhere -- your computer, laptop, iPad folder, email, Google Drive, Dropbox, thumb drive, and even have a hard copy (have pages numbered) with you. Make sure you have everything with you to present in the spirit of excellence.

TRAVEL DOCUMENTS: Days in advance make sure you have all the documents at hand you need to travel smoothly especially if you are traveling overseas -- visa, passport, invitation letters, etc. Don't forget to take pictures of these documents and everything that you are carrying in your wallet. And safe keep them in all the locations we just mentioned above.

SNACKS/FOOD: To avoid spending an exuberant amount of money at airports' restaurants, pack some healthy snacks and sandwiches in case you do encounter unforeseen delays and cancellations.

CONTACT/LOCATION: Make sure you have the address for the venue you are speaking at, the place where you are staying & the contact person's information. It is vital you have this information before leaving home. Also, email and text it to yourself. Please confirm everything as well.

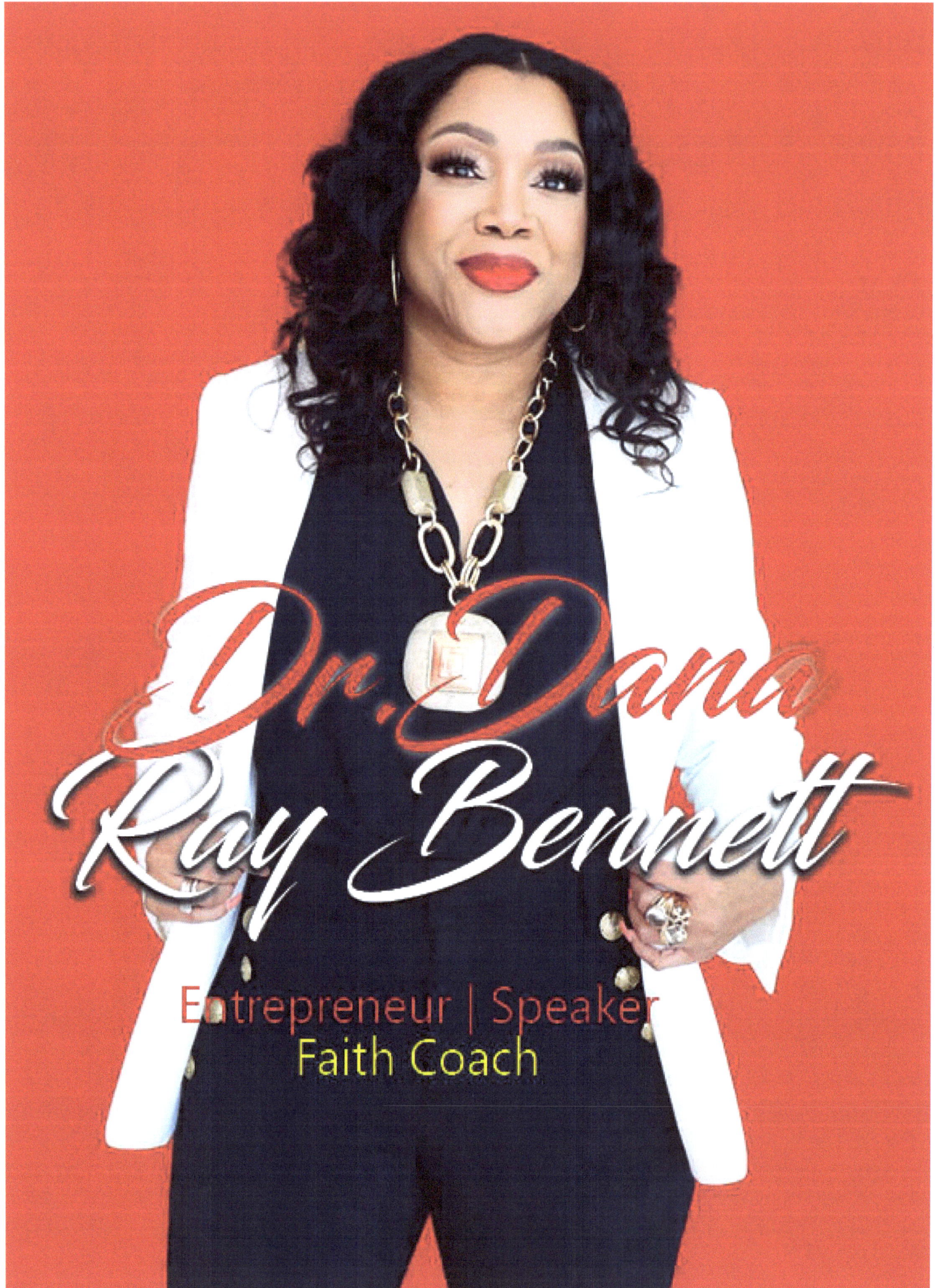

D r. Dana Ray Bennett is the consummate example of a transformative leader who is sincerely and unapologetically dedicated to serving others. She holds a masters in Industrial and Organizational Psychology and a doctorate degree in Christian Business and Leadership. With over 20 years of experience in Corporate America, Dana founded Kingdom, Inc. to help churches, non-profit organizations and small businesses capitalize on proven business strategies. Her expertise spans a variety of specialties to include compliance, risk and leadership development.

Dana is a vocal advocate for women and minorities and believes education and mentorship play a key role in providing opportunities. Out of this conviction, Dana founded and leads Renaissance Christian University (RCU), where the focus is building servant leaders who are kingdom focused and marketplace equipped. Her heart's desire is to provide quality education without the burden of crippling financial debt. To date, RCU has given away over $100k in scholarships and grants to deserving students.

One of her biggest joys is serving in ministry with her husband and family at Connect Church Plano. As a senior leader, Dana is passionate about helping others see the value of living a life dedicated to Christ. Her teaching style is graceful, transparent, witty, challenging, and relevant. She is known for embracing everyone from all walks of life with love and compassion.

Dana counts it an honor to have the opportunity to share via various platforms from boardrooms to pulpits and impact both the marketplace and ministry. She is a wife, mother, business owner, pastor, public speaker, author, coach and leadership strategist.

Contact Info: Drdanabennett@gmail.com

Jabez Bookstore Collection

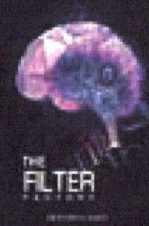

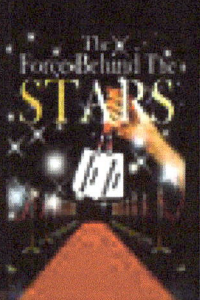

NEED A BOOK PUBLISHED?

Contact: Jabezbooks.com

www.ingramcontent.com/pod-product-compliance
Lightning Source LLC
Chambersburg PA
CBHW042029230526
45474CB00006B/55